2/12

5/17
Lexile: _____

AR/BL: ___6.1___

AR Points: ___1.0___

MONSTER FIGHT CLUB
CREATURES OF MYTHS AND LEGENDS

ANITA GANERI AND DAVID WEST

PowerKiDS
press

New York

Published in 2012 by The Rosen Publishing Group, Inc.
29 East 21st Street, New York, NY 10010

Designed and produced by
David West Books

Designer and illustrator: David West
Editor: Ronne Randall
U.S. Editor: Kara Murray

Photographic credits: 7tr, Sklmsta; 18, Nadia Santoyo; 27, Mike Gil

Library of Congress Cataloging-in-Publication Data

Ganeri, Anita, 1961–
Creatures of myths and legends / by Anita Ganeri and David West.
p. cm. — (Monster fight club)
Includes index.
ISBN 978-1-4488-5198-0 (library binding) — ISBN 978-1-4488-5234-5 (pbk.) —
ISBN 978-1-4488-5235-2 (6-pack)
1. Animals, Mythical—Juvenile literature. 2. Monsters—Juvenile literature. 3. Animals—Folklore. I. West, David, 1956– II. Title.
GR820.G34 2012
398.24'54—dc22

2011007740

Manufactured in China

CPSIA Compliance Information: Batch #DS1102PK:
For Further Information contact Rosen Publishing, New York,
New York at 1-800-237-9932

CONTENTS

INTRODUCTION

Welcome to the Monster Fight Club! Watch as creatures from myth and legend enter the ring to do battle. Have you ever wondered who would win—a horselike hippogriff or a glorious griffin? Find out as you enter their death-defying world.

How Does It Work?

There are six monster fights in this book. Before each fight, you will see a profile page for each contestant. This page gives you more information about them. Once you have read the profile pages, you might be able to take a better guess at who will win the fight.

The profile pages are crammed with fascinating and bloodcurdling facts about each of the contestants.

WARNING

Blood will be spilled!

The illustrations show the contestants in some of their other gory guises.

PROFILE: HIPPOGRIFF

The legendary hippogriff was a creature believed to be the offspring of a griffin and a horse. Hippogriffs were very rare, because griffins and horses were usually enemies, and griffins attacked horses as prey.

Hippogriff Features
A hippogriff was said to have an eagle's head, with sharp talons and powerful, feathered wings. The rest of its body was that of a horse with strong legs and hooves.

A scene from the poem Orlando Furioso, showing a knight riding on a hippogriff.

Riding a Hippogriff
Legend tells how hippogriffs were large, powerful creatures that could fly faster than lightning. They were sometimes tamed and used for riding. The Italian epic poem *Orlando Furioso* was written in the 16th century. In it, Orlando falls in love with a princess, Angelica, but she marries someone else and Orlando goes mad with grief. A knight called Astolfo rides a hippogriff to the moon to bring back Orlando's lost wits. The hippogriff was tamed by a wizard.

Hippogriffs were extremely rare because horses and griffins were usually enemies.

14

PROFILE: GRIFFIN

With the body of a lion and the head and wings of an eagle, a griffin was a powerful beast of legend. Known from China and Central Asia, it was famous for hoarding gold and other treasure, which it defended fiercely.

A griffin on a vase from the Greek city of Eretria, dating from around 350 BC

Magical Powers
In the Middle Ages, griffins were believed to have magical powers. Drinking cups or goblets made from griffin claws or griffin eggs were said to be able to warn of poisoning by changing color if a poisonous liquid had been poured into them. Griffin feathers were also said to be able to cure blindness and were highly valued, though rarely found.

Heraldic Symbols
In art and heraldry, griffins were seen as powerful symbols because they were a cross between a lion, the king of the beasts, and an eagle, the king of the birds. They were used on shields and crests to show strength and courage, combined with intelligence. Female griffins were shown with wings. Male griffins had spines growing from their shoulders.

Griffins are popular as heraldic symbols.

This illustration from Lewis Carroll's Alice in Wonderland shows Alice sitting between a griffin and a mock turtle.

Griffins are smaller than hippogriffs.

15

These large illustrations show you each contestant, warts and all, to give you a good idea of their physical features.

FIGHT 3: HIPPOGRIFF VS. GRIFFIN

In the skies high above a mountain range in Central Asia, two of the most fantastical flying creatures of legend get ready for their fight. Rarely do these two creatures meet, but when they do, feathers are sure to fly. Our two contestants are well matched. Both have strength, courage, and superb flying skills, not to mention razor-sharp talons and beaks. It is far from obvious who will win—the outcome is too close to call.

The griffin has spotted the hippogriff and dives down on it from high in the sky. The hippogriff is unaware of the griffin and cannot see it as it dives out of the sun. At the last minute, the hippogriff spots a shadow and banks to the right. The griffin misses it narrowly. Now the two circle each other, taking advantage of the wind to swoop and glide.

Eyeing each other, silently, neither seems willing to make the first move. Then, suddenly, the griffin lets out an earsplitting shriek and launches another head-on attack.

Screeching and cawing, the two creatures grapple with their sharp talons. Feathers fly as they tear at each other with their hooked beaks. Locked in a deadly embrace, they plummet to the ground. In a desperate attempt to free itself, the griffin uses the claws on its lion's feet to rip at the hippogriff's belly, and the two part, seconds before they hit the ground. As they do, the hippogriff gives a mighty kick with its hooves, catching the griffin in the chest and killing it outright.

STATS
GRIFFIN
AKA Griffon, Gryphon

STRENGTHS: Sharp, hooked beak. Deadly, pointed talons. Powerful wings. Lion's claws. Can defend ferociously.

WEAKNESSES: Hunted by people for its magical body parts.

STATS
HIPPOGRIFF
AKA Hippogryph, Hippogryphe

STRENGTHS: Sharp, hooked beak. Deadly, pointed talons. Powerful wings. Horse's hooves. Can fly faster than the speed of lightning. Faster and stronger than a griffin.

WEAKNESSES: Easier to tame than a griffin.

WINNER: HIPPOGRIFF

16

17

The Monster Fight
After reading the profile pages for each contestant, turn the page to see the fight. Check out the STATS (Statistics) boxes, which give details of the fighters' main strengths and weaknesses. Then read a blow-by-blow account of the battle, if you dare. The winner, if there is one, is shown in a small black box in the bottom right-hand corner.

PROFILE: **CENTAUR**

The great Greek hero Achilles, was taken to Chiron as a child. Chiron became his teacher.

In ancient Greek mythology, centaurs were creatures with the head and upper body of a human, and the legs and lower body of a horse. They were believed to be the sons or grandsons of King Ixion and the cloud nymph Nephele.

Characteristics

According to legend, centaurs had dual personalities. They could be as wild and untamable as horses, but they could also be wise and brave. In addition, they were particularly fond of wine and could behave badly when they had had too much to drink.

Chiron

The most famous of all centaurs was Chiron. Legend said that his father was Cronus, a Titan. Unlike other centaurs, Chiron was intelligent, cultured, and kind. He was also a great healer and teacher, teaching many Greek heroes, such as Achilles, Theseus, and Herakles.

By nature, centaurs are wild but brave and handy with a bow.

Chiron was accidentally shot by Herakles' poisoned arrow. Because he was immortal, he could not die, but he gave up his immortality so that the gods would give people the gift of fire. He was remembered in the sky, as a constellation of stars.

PROFILE: **SCORPION MAN**

A carving showing the Babylonian goddess of healing, Gula, and a scorpion man with the feet of a bird.

Babylonian mythology tells of strange-looking creatures, half human and half animal, called scorpion men. So huge that their heads touched the sky, they had the head, arms, and upper body of a man, and the lower body of a scorpion. These fearsome beings were said to be the children of Tiamat, goddess of the sea. She created them to wage war against the other gods when they betrayed her. They also guarded the mountains where Shamash, the sun god, lived. Deadly warriors, they could fight equally effectively with their scorpion tails, swords, and bows and arrows that never missed their target.

Legends of scorpion men come from the Middle East, where scorpions, such as this black scorpion, are often found.

A scorpion man appears in the famous Epic of Gilgamesh. *It helps the great hero Gilgamesh in his search for immortality.*

This figure of a scorpion man decorates a bronze lid from ancient Egypt.

FIGHT 1: CENTAUR VS. SCORPION

In today's first fight, two mythical creatures that are half beast and half human, encounter one another for the first time somewhere in the Middle East. Caught between two natures—the wise and the wild—the centaur must keep his discipline if he is going to defeat this latest foe. The scorpion man is hardened by years of guarding the abode of the sun god and is used to standing his ground.

The centaur, however, is in the mood for a fight and, throwing caution aside, he approaches his unusual opponent at a gallop. Seeing the wild-eyed creature heading straight toward him at full speed, the scorpion man realizes that he's in for trouble. Quickly, he curls his fearsome, stinging tail over his body in a defensive posture. The centaur slows slightly to fit an arrow in his bow, then fires, but the arrow simply bounces off the scorpion man's armored body. The centaur gallops around the scorpion man, firing arrows as he goes, but all of them suffer the same fate or are deflected by the scorpion man's swords.

STATS

CENTAUR
AKA Sagittarius

STRENGTHS: Fast and strong. Good shot with a bow and arrow.

WEAKNESSES: Very wild, with a short temper. Can be violent. No armor for protection.

MAN

Suddenly, the scorpion man sees his chance. With the centaur's temper getting shorter and shorter, the creature darts out, grabs one of his opponent's legs in his pincers, and draws his sword. The centaur yells in pain and fires an arrow at the human part of the scorpion man, catching him in the shoulder. Surprised, the scorpion man drops his weapons. But he still has hold of the centaur's leg and now grabs another leg in his other pincer. As the centaur struggles, the scorpion man brings down his deadly stinger to sting him. Surely the fight is over now.

But the centaur isn't finished. He drops his bow and grabs the scorpion man's tail. Then, flipping the creature onto his back, the centaur wrestles the scorpion man to the ground. Unable to function properly, the scorpion man releases the centaur from his pincers and concedes defeat.

STATS
SCORPION MAN
AKA Girtablilu, Aqrabuamelu

STRENGTHS: Has eight legs and can scurry and dart remarkably fast. Large pincers are good for grabbing. Has a venomous stinger in his tail. Most of his body is armored. Can fight with swords or a bow and arrow.

WEAKNESSES: His human part is not armored.

WINNER: CENTAUR

PROFILE: **CERBERUS**

A terrifying creature from Greek mythology, Cerberus was a vicious dog who guarded the entrance to the underworld. He is usually shown with three heads, all equipped with sharp, drooling fangs. Cerberus was the offspring of Typhon, a fire-breathing giant, and Echidna, a hideous monster who was half woman and half snake.

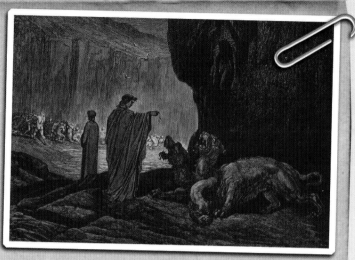

Guard Dog

Cerberus guarded the gates of Hades, the entrance to the underworld, and was the faithful companion of Hades, god of the dead. Cerberus allowed the souls of the dead who had crossed the River Styx to enter but never to leave again. The living were not allowed in, except for Orpheus, who lulled Cerberus to sleep with his lyre.

Cerberus guarded the gates of the underworld to stop the dead from escaping.

Hades gave Herakles permission to catch Cerberus, as long as Herakles did not use any weapons.

Cerberus is usually shown with three heads. He sometimes has a snake's tail.

Capture of Cerberus

One of the 12 tasks that Herakles, the great Greek hero, had to complete was to capture Cerberus alive, without using any weapons. Herakles succeeded and dragged Cerberus out of the underworld. But people were so terrified of the hound that Herakles quickly took him back again.

Herakles killing the Lernaean Hydra. He is wearing his magical lion-skin cloak, which no weapon could pierce.

Another creature from Greek mythology, the Lernaean Hydra was, like Cerberus, the offspring of Typhon and Echidna. It was a huge serpentlike beast, with many heads, and deadly poisonous breath. The Hydra was said to have its lair in Lake Lerna in Greece. Beneath the seemingly calm waters of the lake was another entrance to the underworld, which the Hydra guarded.

A sixteenth-century German illustration of the Hydra

Herakles and the Hydra

Herakles was given the task of killing the Learnaean Hydra, but each time he cut off one of its heads, two more heads grew in its place. Herakles called on his nephew Ioalus for help.

Each time Herakles cut off a head, Ioalus sealed the stump with a burning branch so that it could not grow back again.

The Hydra had the same parents as Cerberus, the three-headed dog.

FIGHT 2: CERBERUS VS. THE

Today's contestants have a great deal in common. Both are many-headed monsters guarding the gates of hell. But their connection goes deeper than that. They are, in fact, closely related—both are the offspring of a giant and a snake-woman—but there is not much love lost between them.

On a day off, Cerberus strolls around Lake Lerna, looking to reenter the underworld.

STATS
CERBERUS
AKA Kerberos

STRENGTHS: Fierce, three-headed hellhound. Razor-sharp fangs. Sometimes shown with a snake's tail.

WEAKNESSES: Can be captured by a hero, even without weapons.

LERNAEAN HYDRA

He finds his path blocked by the Hydra—the fight is on. With a snarl that sounds three times, Cerberus, the hellhound, launches himself at the sinister serpent. At first, the Hydra is taken by surprise and beats a hasty retreat back to its lair. Cerberus leaps onto its back and prepares to bite. But the Hydra's scaly skin is too tough even for this demon dog's razor-sharp fangs. Leaping to the ground, Cerberus decides to tackle the Hydra head on. In a breathtaking feat of viciousness, he rips off one head—only to find that two immediately grow back in its place.

Cerberus launches another attack, but the result is the same. Faced with so many heads, the dog's dismay soon turns to terror. As head after head belches out deadly fumes, he soon finds himself overwhelmed by the Hydra's poisonous breath. He also swallowed a large amount of the Hydra's poisonous blood when he bit its heads off. Before long, he is lying on the ground, breathing his last.

STATS
THE LERNAEAN HYDRA
AKA The Hydra of Lerna

STRENGTHS: Deadly poisonous breath and blood. Even its tracks are poisonous. Can grow two heads if one head is chopped off.

WEAKNESSES: Can be killed by heroes.

WINNER: THE LERNAEAN HYDRA

PROFILE: **HIPPOGRIFF**

The legendary hippogriff was a creature believed to be the offspring of a griffin and a horse. Hippogriffs were very rare, because griffins and horses were usually enemies, and griffins attacked horses as prey.

Hippogriff Features

A hippogriff was said to have an eagle's head, with sharp talons and powerful, feathered wings. The rest of its body was that of a horse with strong legs and hooves.

A scene from the poem Orlando Furioso, *showing a knight riding on a hippogriff*

Hippogriffs were extremely rare because horses and griffins were usually enemies.

Riding a Hippogriff

Legend tells how hippogriffs were large, powerful creatures that could fly faster than lightning. They were sometimes tamed and used for riding. The Italian epic poem *Orlando Furioso* was written in the 16th century. In it, Orlando falls in love with a princess, Angelica, but she marries someone else and Orlando goes mad with grief. A knight called Astolfo rides a hippogriff to the moon to bring back Orlando's lost wits. The hippogriff was tamed by a wizard.

PROFILE: **GRIFFIN**

With the body of a lion and the head and wings of an eagle, a griffin was a powerful beast of legend. Known from China and Central Asia, it was famous for hoarding gold and other treasure, which it defended fiercely.

A griffin on a vase from the Greek city of Eretria, dating from around 350 BC

Magical Powers

In the Middle Ages, griffins were believed to have magical powers. Drinking cups or goblets made from griffin claws or griffin eggs were said to be able to warn of poisoning by changing color if a poisonous liquid had been poured into them. Griffin feathers were also said to be able to cure blindness and were highly valued, though rarely found.

Griffins are popular as heraldic symbols.

Heraldic Symbols

In art and heraldry, griffins were seen as powerful symbols because they were a cross between a lion, the king of the beasts, and an eagle, the king of the birds. They were used on shields and crests to show strength and courage, combined with intelligence. Female griffins were shown with wings. Male griffins had spines growing from their shoulders.

This illustration from Lewis Carroll's Alice in Wonderland *shows Alice sitting between a griffin and a mock turtle.*

Griffins are smaller than hippogriffs.

15

FIGHT 3: HIPPOGRIFF VS. GRIFFIN

In the skies high above a mountain range in Central Asia, two of the most fantastical flying creatures of legend get ready for their fight. Rarely do these two creatures meet, but when they do, feathers are sure to fly. Our two contestants are well matched. Both have strength, courage, and superb flying skills, not to mention razor-sharp talons and beaks. It is far from obvious who will win—the outcome is too close to call.

The griffin has spotted the hippogriff and dives down on it from high in the sky. The hippogriff is unaware of the griffin and cannot see it as it dives out of the sun. At the last minute, the hippogriff spots a shadow and banks to the right. The griffin misses it narrowly. Now the two circle each other, taking advantage of the wind to swoop and glide.

STATS

HIPPOGRIFF
AKA Hippogryph, Hippogryphe

STRENGTHS: Sharp, hooked beak. Deadly, pointed talons. Powerful wings. Horse's hooves. Can fly faster than the speed of lightning. Faster and stronger than a griffin.

WEAKNESSES: Easier to tame than a griffin.

GRIFFIN
AKA Griffon, Gryphon

STRENGTHS: Sharp, hooked beak. Deadly, pointed talons. Powerful wings. Lion's claws. Can defend ferociously.

WEAKNESSES: Hunted by people for its magical body parts.

Eyeing each other, silently, neither seems willing to make the first move. Then, suddenly, the griffin lets out an earsplitting shriek and launches another head-on attack.

Screeching and cawing, the two creatures grapple with their sharp talons. Feathers fly as they tear at each other with their hooked beaks. Locked in a deadly embrace, they plummet to the ground. In a desperate attempt to free itself, the griffin uses the claws on its lion's feet to rip at the hippogriff's belly, and the two part, seconds before they hit the ground. As they do, the hippogriff gives a mighty kick with its hooves, catching the griffin in the chest and killing it outright.

WINNER: HIPPOGRIFF

PROFILE: **CHUPACABRA**

The terrrifying chupacabra is a legendary creature from Latin America. Said to look like a cross between a kangaroo and a dog, it has scaly, hairless skin, horns, fanglike teeth, and a row of long, sharp spines running along its back.

The preserved remains of animals thought to be chupacabras have been displayed in traveling fairs.

Goat Sucker

The chupacabra's name means "goat sucker," after its habit of preying on animals like goats and sheep. It catches its victim in its razor-sharp claws and sucks its blood through a series of small, round puncture wounds.

Sinister Sightings

There have been many supposed sightings of chupacabras, including many recent ones. Many were reported by farmers who found that their livestock had been killed and drained of their blood. Most described the creature as being doglike with leathery skin and fangs. It was later found that some of these creatures were, in fact, coyotes suffering from a disease called mange.

The chupacabra is said to suck blood from its victims, like a vampire.

PROFILE: **MANTICORE**

The myth of the manticore orginally came from Persia, where its name meant "man-eater." It passed into European legend through the work of a Greek writer who claimed that this ferocious-looking beast was also to be found in India and other parts of Asia.

Manticore Features

According to the legend, a manticore had the body of a lion, with red fur; the face of a human; and three rows of sharp, sharklike teeth. It ranged in size from that of a lion to that of a horse. A manticore usually had lion's paws but sometimes had dragon's feet. Its tail ended in a club made of poisonous spines that it could shoot out to paralyze or kill its prey of monkeys, deer, and humans. It was known to devour its prey whole, leaving no trace behind.

This illustration of a manticore appears in a book about legendary beasts from the thirteenth century.

Disappearances

In parts of Asia, the manticore is thought to be terrifyingly real. If a person goes missing in mysterious circumstances, it is believed that a manticore has eaten him.

The manticore was said to have a loud, trumpetlike voice.

FIGHT 4: CHUPACABRA VS.

A monstrous manticore has escaped from a freak show currently touring the villages and towns of Central America. And it's hungry. Feasting mainly on unwary travelers, lured to its lair by the sound of its trumpetlike voice, it has unexpectedly attracted the attention of an equally rare and equally hideous chupacabra. The sight of the unwanted guest sends the red monster into a rage. It raises its tail and fires off a couple of poisonous spines that pierce the chupacabra's leathery skin. The chupacabra hisses and screeches in alarm, and its eyes glow a terrifying red. The fight is definitely on. The two beasts charge each other in a ferocious

STATS
CHUPACABRA
AKA Goat sucker

STRENGTHS: Heavy. Sharp teeth and claws. Leathery skin and spines along its back give some protection.

WEAKNESSES: Drinks blood.

MANTICORE

show of strength. Hopping on its back legs, the chupacabra lunges at the manticore with its knife-sharp claws. It opens its mouth wide, ready to take a bite with its fangs. But the manticore gets there first, and uses its sharklike teeth to rips a gash in the chupacabra's shoulder. Roaring in pain, the chupacabra gouges a chunk out of the manticore's side and prepares to drain it of its blood.

But time is running out for the chupacabra. The deadly poison from the manticore's tail spines is beginning to do its work. As the chupacabra weakens, all that is left is for the manticore to devour it, leaving not a morsel behind.

STATS
MANTICORE
AKA Man-eater

STRENGTHS: Powerful body of a lion. Three rows of sharklike teeth. Can shoot poisonous spines from its tail.

WEAKNESSES: Can be easily seen and heard.

WINNER: MANTICORE

21

PROFILE: **KRAKEN**

For centuries, sailors were terrified by tales of sea monsters that attacked and swallowed up ships. Among the most feared was the legendary kraken, a creature of immense size that was said to live off the coast of Scandinavia.

Kraken Features

Early accounts described the kraken as being the size of a large island. It had huge, flailing tentacles and a sharp, stabbing beak. It lived at great depths, rarely rising from the seabed. More dangerous than the kraken itself was the deadly whirlpool it generated when it dived back down again, dragging ships down with it.

An illustration of a reported attack by a kraken in the early nineteenth century

Giant Squid?

The legend of the kraken may be based in fact. It may have originated from sightings of giant squid which are thought to grow to around 45 feet (14 m) long. Very little is known about this extraordinary animal because only a few have been found.

The kraken may have been based on sailors' tales of seeing giant squid.

Descriptions of the kraken are limited to its tentacles and vast size. It was said to create a dangerous whirlpool when it dived back down into the sea.

PROFILE: **LEVIATHAN**

An illustration showing the Leviathan as a dragonlike beast

Another monstrous sea creature was the Leviathan, which is described in the Bible. In particular, its name has come to mean any enormous, whalelike beast, but other legends refer to an animal that looks like a cross between a giant serpent and a crocodile.

Leviathan Features

The Leviathan was described as the world's largest creature, its back covered in rows of shields. Its eyes flashed with a brilliant light, and fire and smoke poured out of its mouth and nostrils. When it was hungry, its breath made the sea boil. It was so strong that it could not be harmed by arrows, and it left a boiling whirlpool in its wake. Its mouth was huge, and filled with fearsome teeth, like a gateway to hell.

The Leviathan's mouth was said to be a gateway to hell.

The Leviathan, with two other monsters from Jewish mythology—Behemoth, the land monster; and Ziz, monster of the air

An image of the whalelike Leviathan, with its huge body and rows of shields on its back. Reports of this creature may have been based on sightings of whales.

23

FIGHT 5: KRAKEN VS. LEVIATHAN

Down in the depths of the ocean, two great sea monsters are stirring. Both are of gigantic size, and both are hungry. The Leviathan is on the lookout for a tasty whale to eat when it suddenly spies a larger and perhaps more succulent meal in the shape of the kraken. It does not strike immediately, but bides its time while it observes its potential prey. In its hunt for food, the kraken has begun to move toward the surface of the ocean, where it hopes to find a warship and its crew. The Leviathan makes its move. With its enormous mouth gaping open, it looms out of the gloom, causing the water to boil with its fiery breath.

It is surprising that these two colossal contestants have not encountered each other before. But they have so far managed to keep their distance in the vast reaches of the deep. It is no wonder then that the kraken is taken by surprise as it sees the Leviathan approaching. In an attempt to escape its attacker's gigantic jaws, the kraken shoots out a cloud of black ink and heads back down, leaving a whirling pool of water behind. But this does not stop the Leviathan, which closes in and grasps the kraken in its mouth. The kraken wraps its tentacles around the giant, scraping deep wounds into its flesh with its hooked suckers. The Leviathan's grip weakens slightly, just enough to let the kraken escape...

STATS
LEVIATHAN
AKA Hellmouth

STRENGTHS:
Hundreds of miles long. Can boil the ocean with its breath. Shields on back. Supernatural strength.

WEAKNESSES: Will be overcome at the end of time. Afraid of a small worm called a kilbit.

...squirting its last reserves of ink behind it. The Leviathan, though, follows the ink trail and almost reaches the slippery kraken. Before it can bite, a small worm called a kilbit swims out of the kraken's gill covers. Despite its size, the Leviathan is terrified of this tiny creature and backs away in fear. The kraken seizes its chance and attacks, but the kilbit has swum away and the Leviathan lunges. It bites the kraken in two and gulps both pieces down.

STATS
KRAKEN

STRENGTHS: Has many limbs with suckers. Giant. Sharp beak. Ink sac. Can sink ships.

WEAKNESSES: Lightweight, compared with the Leviathan.

WINNER: LEVIATHAN

PROFILE: **WESTERN DRAGON**

A huge lizardlike beast with scaly skin that breathes fire or poison—this is the typical image of a Western dragon. Famous from European folklore, these creatures were said to hatch from eggs, like reptiles, and to live for hundreds of years.

Dragons are used as heraldic symbols, such as this one on the flag of Wales.

Dragon Habits

Unlike their Eastern counterparts, Western dragons were usually seen as dangerous, terrorizing towns and villages and demanding human sacrifices.

Western dragons had four legs and two large, leathery wings. They breathed fire.

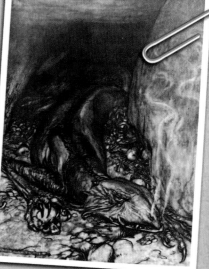

At other times, they lived in remote mountain or sea caves where they guarded their hoards of treasure—gold and precious stones. Anyone who dared to try to steal a dragon's hoard was unlikely to come back alive.

In its mountain lair, the dragon Fafnir guarded its hoard of gold until it was killed by Sigurd.

Hero Bait

There are many tales of great heroes who tried to slay dragons. In Norse mythology, Sigurd killed the dragon Fafnir with his magical sword, Gram, and seized the creature's gold. Then Sigurd bathed in the dragon's blood, which made him invulnerable, except for a small place on his shoulder.

St. George was a famous dragon slayer. He killed a dragon to rescue a princess.

PROFILE: EASTERN DRAGON

Eastern dragons were huge and powerful creatures, but unlike Western dragons, they were benevolent beasts that tried to help people. For this reason, they were treated with great respect in many Eastern cultures. These dragons were also serpentlike with a covering of scales and spikes. They sometimes had long whiskers and horns on their heads. They did not have wings, but were believed to use their magic to fly instead.

Rulers of Nature

Eastern dragons were often worshipped for their great wisdom and as rulers of nature. In particular, they were believed to control water and to have power over rainfall, storms, and the seas.

Eastern dragons were usually good-natured, but in a Japanese story, the hero Susanoo killed an evil dragon called Yamata no Orochi.

In Chinese mythology, there were four dragon kings, each representing one of the four seas. Temples were dedicated to them, and sacrifices made to them.

Chinese Dragons

In China, dragons have for centuries been seen as symbols of strength and good luck. An outstanding person was often compared to a dragon, a noble creature. A dragon was also the symbol of the Chinese emperor, and the imperial throne was called the Dragon Throne.

The Chinese dragon was called a lung *and was usually found in an underwater cave or lair. The number of toes on its feet varied from three to five. It had horns, teeth, and claws, which it used to defend itself from attack.*

FIGHT 6: WESTERN DRAGON

Blown off course by strong winds, an Eastern dragon finds itself in Europe. It has accidentally strayed into the territory of a Western dragon that has built up an impressive hoard of gold and treasure. When it sees the exotic intruder flying close by, the Western dragon launches itself into the air, aggressively breathing out fire. The Eastern dragon is taken by surprise—it is not used to such violent behavior. It turns and begins to fly away over the towers of the local town.

But the Western dragon does not give up so easily. It attacks its unsuspecting visitor with a hot blast from its jaws. The Eastern dragon tries to veer away from the heat, knocking slates and bricks from the top of a tower. Then it summons up a violent storm and quickly puts out its opponent's fire. Before the bedraggled Western dragon can regroup, the Eastern dragon turns into a hurricane and blows it far out to sea.

STATS
WESTERN DRAGON
AKA European dragon, Knucker

STRENGTHS: Has wings and can fly. Very aggressive, especially when guarding its treasure. Can spit out fire or poison. Sharp teeth and claws.

WEAKNESSES: Very possessive of treasure. Can be slain by great heroes.

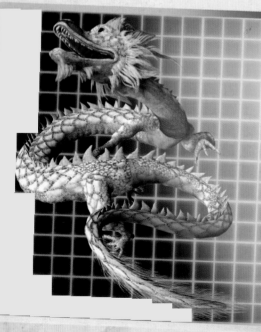

STATS
EASTERN DRAGON
AKA Chinese dragon, Lung

STRENGTHS: Can form clouds and summon storms. Can turn into water, change color, and glow in the dark.

WEAKNESSES: Good-natured, so is rarely aggressive.

Flapping its wings ever more frantically, the Western dragon is no match for the storm. As it struggles to head back to shore, and its hoard of treasure, the wind keeps blowing it back to sea again. It will take the Western dragon a few days to find its way back home, if it ever can. In the meantime, the Eastern dragon is declared the winner of the fight.

VS. EASTERN DRAGON

WINNER: EASTERN DRAGON

CREATE YOUR OWN FIGHT

You might not agree with some of the fight results in this book. If that's the case, try writing your own fight report based on the facts supplied on the prefight profile pages. Better still, choose your own mythical creatures and create your own fight.

Monster Research

Once you have chosen your two mythical creatures, do some research about them using books and the Internet. You can make them fairly similar, like the hippogriff and the griffin, or quite different, like Cerberus and the Hydra.

Stats Boxes

Think about stats for each creature. Find out about any other names for the AKA section. Make a list of strengths, such as how powerful they are, and if they have magic armor or supernatural features. Also list any weaknesses.

In the Ring

Pick a setting where your creatures are likely to meet, and write a blow-by-blow account of how you imagine the fight might happen. Think of each contestant's key characteristics, along with its strengths and weaknesses. Remember, there doesn't always have to be a winner.

Creatures of Myths and Legends

Here's a list of some other creatures that might qualify for membership in the Monster Fight Club:

Baku
Cockatrice
Bigfoot
Bunyip
Cyclops
Kappa
Kitsune
Mermaid
Minotaur
Naga
Nuckelavee
Phoenix
Quetzalcoatl
Tengu

A cockatrice can turn a person to stone with its stare.

GLOSSARY

benevolent (beh-NEV-lent)
Kindly and friendly, doing good rather than evil.

constellation (kon-stuh-LAY-shun)
A group of stars in the sky.

epic (EH-pik)
A long poem that tells of the deeds of a great hero.

gill covers (GIL KUH-verz)
Flaplike covers that protect the gills (body parts used for breathing) of fish and many other sea creatures.

hoard (HAWRD)
A store of treasure, money or jewels, hidden away for use in the future.

hoarding (HAWR-ding)
Gathering or collecting a store of treasure and hiding it for use in the future.

immortal (ih-MAWR-tul)
Someone who never dies but lives for ever.

imperial (im-PEER-ee-ul)
To do with an empire or an emperor.

invulnerable (in-VUL-neh-ruh-bel)
Not able to be wounded, hurt or damaged.

lair (LER)
The resting or hiding place of a wild animal.

legend (LEH-jend)
A traditional story that is often based in an event that is supposedly historical.

lyre (LYR)
A musical instrument from ancient Greece. It was made from a tortoise shell.

mange (MAYNJ)
A disease that can affect dogs and other animals, causing their skin to itch and their hair to fall out.

mythology (mih-THAH-luh-jee)
A collection of myths or traditional stories that use supernatural characters to explain human behavior and natural events.

nymph (NIMF)
A spirit of nature in ancient Greek mythology who often appeared as a young woman.

prey (PRAY)
An animal that is hunted and killed by another animal for food.

venomous (VEH-nuh-mis)
Another word for poisonous.

INDEX

Web Sites

Due to the changing nature of Internet links, PowerKids Press has developed an online list of Web sites related to the subject of this book. This site is updated regularly. Please use this link to access the list:
www.powerkidslinks.com/mfc/myth/